Original title:
Slicing the Orange

Copyright © 2025 Creative Arts Management OÜ
All rights reserved.

Author: Tobias Winslow
ISBN HARDBACK: 978-1-80586-441-7
ISBN PAPERBACK: 978-1-80586-913-9

The Sweetness Within

A fruit so bright, it makes me grin,
Peel it back and dive right in,
Juices flying, oh what a scene,
Sticky fingers in between.

Seeds like confetti, a playful surprise,
I squint and laugh at the citrus skies,
Each slice resembles a tiny sun,
Who knew this fruit could be such fun?

A Mosaic of Flavor

In a bowl of sunshine, colors collide,
Each wedge a treasure, bursting with pride,
A palette of sweetness, tangy and bright,
I giggle as I take my first bite.

Juice drips down like a tiny stream,
I chase it with laughter and a dream,
No need for a knife, I'm living the life,
This fruity escapade reduces all strife.

Tangy Revelations

Bright orbs in a pile, what do they hide?
A zesty surprise, go on and decide,
One bite takes you on a rollercoaster ride,
Who knew a fruit could be such a guide?

With every squirt, a giggle ensues,
The tangy explosion, a laugh that ensues,
I'm a citrus ninja, on a juicy quest,
Making a mess? Oh, I'm feeling blessed!

The Fragrance of Dusk

As evening falls, the scent fills the air,
A citrus perfume, beyond compare,
With each zest, the day's worries fade,
A comedic delight, in this fruity parade.

Friends gather 'round with a slice in hand,
Laughter erupts, it's perfectly planned,
We toast to the tang, to the vibrant hue,
In this juicy world, there's room for a few!

Juices of Dusk

As the sun dips, colors blend,
A fruity battle, who will bend?
With sticky hands and laughter loud,
We juice the dusk, we're feeling proud.

Citrus dribbles down our chins,
The sweetest war, let the fun begin!
A twist of fate, a punchline slips,
We squirt our jokes, no need for scripts.

Segments of Sunrise

Morning rays and juicy bites,
Tangled up in citrus fights.
We toss the halves, they roll and spin,
Oh what a mess, let the fun begin!

A grapefruit splat, a lemon ping,
Each morning's battle's quite the thing.
With oranges flying, we take a chance,
In the zesty chaos, we laugh and dance.

The Zest Between Us

In the kitchen, we take our stand,
With fruity armor, a brave band.
We trade our peels with giddy glee,
Zesty jokes bounce, just wait and see!

A tangerine toss, a giggle's sound,
A citrus circus, round and round.
Juice flies high, splatters like paint,
In this zesty mess, no room for restraint.

Citrus Dreams

In dreams of zest, we juice and play,
With giggles quick, we'll save the day.
Lemonade pools in the backyard sun,
In this fruity world, we all have fun!

A clementine slide, a tangerine swing,
We're laughing loud at silly things.
Adventures ripe in every peel,
In citrus dreams, we spin the wheel.

The Citrus Canvas Palette

With every cut, a splash of zest,
A canvas bright, in nature's quest.
Juicy drips like artists' paint,
Creating smiles, without restraint.

A twist and turn, oh what a thrill,
Sticky fingers, couldn't keep still.
Lemon frowns, a limey grin,
Each citrus tale about to begin.

Treasures Held Within

Orbs of sunshine in a bowl,
Hidden gems, our sweet control.
Peel the skin and laugh aloud,
Juicy treasures, proud and loud.

In every wedge, a pop of cheer,
Pips of fun, my dear sincere.
Each bite a burst, a citrus spree,
With friends around, it's heaven, see?

Glories of the Hour on the Board

Board of joy, with colors bright,
Citrus globe in wondrous sight.
Friends gather round, a happy chime,
Chopping here, we bide our time.

With laughter shared and juice that drips,
We toast our joy with all these nips.
Every wedge, a slice of fun,
Our fruity feast has just begun.

The Yield of Luminous Cuts

A dance of hands, the fruit is split,
Artful wedges, each a hit.
Bright segments shine like summer days,
In citrus laughter, we're all ablaze.

Giggles rise with every cut,
Pucker up, but never shut!
We savor bites, oh what a treat,
Citrusy chaos, oh so sweet.

Sacred Rituals of Peeling

In the kitchen, all set with glee,
A fruit that's bright, calling to me.
I grab a knife, but it slips right down,
Oh, sticky fingers, wear my crown!

The zest flies high like a wild balloon,
It dances around, a citrus tune.
With every twist, I think of my fate,
Did I call this fruit, or did it debate?

A Burst of Flavor in Every Bite

The moment comes, I take a taste,
A juicy squirt, oh what a waste!
Like a fountain that greets my chin,
A citrus shower, let's begin!

Each bite's a giggle, friends gather near,
Those sunny slices, oh so dear.
We laugh and slurp, it's pure delight,
Citrus joy, we savor the night!

Sweet and Sour Confessions

In the realm of fruit, I stand confound,
Sweetness mocks me, tartness astounds.
One bite of joy, the next a cringe,
A flavor clash, I start to binge.

I confess my love, despite the fight,
These zesty curves bring me pure light.
With every nibble, my heart takes flight,
A funny dance, a citrus delight!

Stardust in Citrus Rind

In my hand, a globe of sun,
What's inside? Oh, this is fun!
Peel away layers, a cosmic show,
Glittery zest, like stars that glow.

Tangled in pith, a messy spree,
This fruit's a jester, wild and free.
Its laughter bursts with every bite,
A comical feast, under moonlight!

Golden Geometry of Nature

In the garden, shapes align,
A circle here, a line divine.
Peeling back the sunny skin,
Who knew snacks could make us grin?

Juicy wedges stacked just right,
In my hand, a sweet delight.
Look out, world, I'm quite the chef,
With every bite, I'm laughing left!

Citrus Cascades on Canvas

Orange paint splashed on my shirt,
A masterpiece made from fruity flirt.
Brush strokes of zest flying free,
This art's as messy as can be!

My palette's bursting with bright cheer,
Nature's laughs ring loud and clear.
Droplets dance in the sun's warm glow,
Caught in giggles, watch them flow!

Threads of Taste in Every Slice

Strands of flavor, woven well,
A tapestry of taste to tell.
Each cut reveals a vibrant hue,
Not just a snack, it's fun for two!

Threads of sweetness, tangy flair,
A citrus circus in the air.
Juggling flavors, let them fly,
In this zesty pie, we laugh and sigh!

Sunbeams Drenched in Juice

Golden globes beneath the sun,
A juicy mess, oh what fun!
Sticky fingers, laughter spills,
Every drop, a joy that thrills.

Sunbeam-chasers, we unite,
Chasing happiness in each bite.
A splash of zest upon my face,
Life's a laugh in this bright space!

A Slice of Radiance

In the sunlit kitchen, I make my stand,
An orb in hand, it's simply grand.
With a twist and a turn, I give it a go,
Juice flies like confetti, oh what a show!

Zesty droplets dance, oh what a mess,
Leave it to fruit to cause such distress.
The cat leaps back, a wild-eyed stare,
Is it a feast or a juicy nightmare?

The Tangy Tapestry

Colors galore in a fruity parade,
Peeling and slicing, my hands have obeyed.
The zest fills the room, with giggles so bright,
Even the dog thinks it's a taste bud delight!

I wear a crown of pulp on my head,
The segments are laughing, oh what have I said?
A fruit fiasco, a juicer's dream,
In this kitchen circus, we burst at the seam!

Juice Drips from the Horizon

A bright orb perched on my kitchen ledge,
I take a deep breath, stand up to the edge.
With a dance of delight and a playful roar,
The citrus explosion, can't ask for more!

Dribbles and drops leave trails on my face,
I'm half-spinning, half-slick in this zesty race.
Each squirt a giggle, each splash a cheer,
Juice drips in laughter, we've nothing to fear!

The First Cut Reveals Brightness

I reach for the orb, shining with glee,
The first cut, a giggle, oh what will it be?
It splits like a joke, and the laughter flows,
In citrus delight, everyone knows!

Squeezed chaos spills, like sunshine on fries,
Unpredictable giggles, like clouds in the skies.
Mom's got a towel, the dog's in a race,
As we savor the warmth of this fruity embrace!

Spiral of Taste

In the kitchen, chaos reigns,
Citrus bits fly like planes.
Juice squirts across the floor,
Laughter echoes, who could ask for more?

A fruit in hand, a grin so wide,
With each twist, zesty juice will slide.
Orange segments, bright and bold,
A comedy of colors, pure gold.

Peeling back, oh what a sight,
Juicy treasures feel just right.
Who knew fruit could be such fun?
We'll keep this party, never done!

So here we stand, fruit in tow,
Hilarity blooms like a citrus show.
With every bite, giggles unfurl,
A sweet little mess, our joyful world.

Citrus Symphony

Sound of laughter fills the air,
As citrus spills from everywhere.
Zesty notes, a fruity tune,
Dancing in the afternoon.

Fingers slip on orange skin,
A riot of colors, let the fun begin.
Sweet and tangy, a flavor spree,
In this symphony, just you and me.

Juicy droplets, they cascade,
Creating puddles, a citrus parade.
While we juggle, and citrus flies,
Each slice brings great surprise.

When life gives oranges, we shall sing,
For in this chaos, joy does spring.
With every bite and silly dance,
We've found our zest in this wild chance.

The Art of Peeling

Behold the fruit, a masterpiece,
A citrus canvas, never cease.
With fingers poised, the peeling starts,
Art in the kitchen, warming our hearts.

Layers fall like old regrets,
Juicy treasures, no regrets.
A twist, a tug, with playful glee,
Who knew fruit could bring such glee?

Chopping sounds create a beat,
The kitchen floor is now a treat.
Orange petals fly away,
Life's best moments often stray.

So gather 'round, let's make a mess,
In this peeling art, we're truly blessed.
With laughter here, we'll boldly claim,
The citrus joy in this crazy game.

Harmony of Hues

In a bowl, the orange gleams,
Under sunlight, it beams.
Colors clash, a vibrant fight,
Bringing smiles with sheer delight.

Fingers slip, the peel unfolds,
A juicy treasure, stories told.
Like a painter with a brush,
Creating joy in every rush.

Squeezed and squished, it makes a splash,
Juicy laughter, a perfect clash.
Segments wink in playful style,
Each bite a burst, stay awhile.

So gather friends, let's break the fruit,
In this harmony, we'll all salute.
For in each twist and every squeeze,
Laughter blooms like summer breeze.

Sweetly Curved Bliss

In the kitchen, what a sight,
A fruit with cheer and vibrant light.
One twist, one turn, a squirt to face,
Potential chaos in this fruity race.

Citrus zest all around the floor,
Peeled skin flying—what a score!
Giggles echo as drops cascade,
This juicy game we gladly played.

Bright drops land on the old cat's nose,
He sneezes and leaps with cheeky prose.
Each bite bursts like confetti fun,
In this mad kitchen, laughter's spun.

So grab a fork and dig right in,
A tangy battle? Let the fun begin!
Sweetly curved joy on every tray,
In our zesty world, we laugh and play.

The Elixir of Radiance

A golden orb with sunny hue,
Cradled gently, bright as dew.
Open it up, a little fight,
Juicy treasures—oh, what a sight!

Wobbling on the counter's edge,
Could it roll off—oh, we pledge!
Giggles rise with every squirt,
A citrus shower—then the dirt!

Laughter fills this buzzing space,
As sticky fingers embrace the race.
A glass is filled, we take a sip,
The tangy goodness on our lips.

With each gulp, we dance and sway,
This bubbling joy just won't decay.
An elixir bright, our spirits soar,
Radiant laughter—who could ask for more?

Nature's Tangy Whisper

In the orchard, whispers play,
Nature's gift in bright display.
Plucked from trees with zestful cheer,
A sweet surprise that draws us near.

With a wink, it rolls away,
Chasing shadows—come, let's play!
The ground is splashed with liquid sun,
Nature's fun means there's always one!

Wrapped in peel, it hides its spark,
Unleash the burst—oh, what a lark!
A tangy bite, a juicy laugh,
This fruity joy, we'll cut in half.

As we share, don't miss a drop,
Each dribble's worth a giggle pop!
Nature's dance on our plates unfolds,
In this tangy bliss, our laughter molds.

Soft Cuts of Summer's Smile

Soft slices on a wooden board,
Sunshine giggles and joy outpoured.
Every piece a bright surprise,
With zesty laughs, we harmonize.

Laughter bounces, bright and free,
As we tackle this tangy spree.
One slice rolls, the floor's a mess,
But oh, who cares? We wouldn't stress!

Juicy treasures slide and land,
Sticky fingers go hand in hand.
The summer sun shines warm and bright,
As we snack and savor the light.

Let's share a toast—your glass, mine too,
With each sip, we feel renewed.
Soft cuts bring happiness our way,
In summer's glow, we laugh and play.

Rind and Reverie

In the kitchen, what a sight,
An orange rolls into the light.
With a knife, oh what a thrill,
Fruit confetti, I can't keep still.

Peel it back, like a magician's act,
Juicy surprises, that's a fact.
Slice by slice, giggles ensue,
Citrus laughter, just for you.

Sticky fingers, a comic scene,
Tropical juice, a fruity sheen.
Rind on the floor, a slippery fate,
Watch your step, don't tempt fate!

In the end, a juicy grin,
Who knew that chaos could begin?
With each chunk, our laughter grows,
Orange antics steal the show!

Nature's Geometry

Round and orange, let's take a look,
A fruit so bright, it's like a book.
With angles sharp, and curves so fine,
Making fun shapes, like a cartoon line.

Peeling back layers, a zestful twist,
In this funny dance, you can't resist.
Every wedge a playful tease,
Watch them roll, with citrus ease.

A juggling act, it slips, it slides,
Round and round, where laughter hides.
Juice drips down, a sticky plight,
Nature's joke, pure delight!

So here we stand, with a grin so wide,
In fruity joy, we'll take our ride.
Nature's geometry, oh so sweet,
Who knew fruit could be such a treat?

Unpeeling the Sun

There it sits, a globe so bright,
In my kitchen, oh what a sight.
Peel it back like a treasure map,
Citrus surprise, a juicy clap!

With every twist, a giggle bursts,
Each segment holds a zestful thirst.
Like sunbeams in a sticky fight,
Who knew fruit could be such light?

Chunks of joy that pop and roll,
Slippery fun, a playful goal.
Juice spews forth, a sunny spray,
Nature's laughter on display!

In the bowl, a cheerful mess,
Sticky hands, I must confess.
Unpeeling joy, day by day,
With a smile, I'll always play!

Fragments of Flavor

In the bowl, they dance around,
Juicy gems in colors found.
With a slice here, a bite so sweet,
Laughter echoes with every treat.

Oh! A wedge goes flying by,
Citrus giggles fill the sky.
With friends we munch, our spirits high,
Juicy fragments make us sigh.

Juice-splash battles, what a game,
Who knew fruit could hold such fame?
In each segment, a fruity tease,
A sweet twist brings us to our knees.

So here's to fun, and laughter bright,
In our kitchen, in morning light.
Fragments of flavor, a playful tune,
Savor the joy, hum a happy rune!

Juicy Echoes of Past

Once a fruit with a vibrant glow,
Rolling on the kitchen floor, oh no!
The dog chased it with gleeful yelps,
While Auntie laughed, she's a bit like kelp.

Sticky hands and juice that drips,
Children dive for citrus sips,
A splatter here, a giggle there,
Mom grumbles, "Oh, please beware!"

Neighbors peek from behind the gate,
Curious about our fruity fate,
As we dance around, big grins abound,
Each zesty burst brings more joy to sound.

And though the citrus found its end,
It lives on in tales we love to send,
Juicy echoes that won't depart,
Forever cheerful in our heart.

Segmented Bliss under a Bright Sky

On a picnic blanket, we lay sprawled,
The sun blaring like a trumpet walled,
A fruit parade upon our spread,
Each piece a burst, no worries ahead.

Grandpa juggles, what a sight!
With orange halves that fly left and right,
A twist, a turn, they land in place,
But splats and laughs fill up the space.

A seagull swoops, what a crow!
Stealing bites from the show below,
We shriek and shout, what a near miss!
Citrus chaos, too funny to dismiss.

Under the sky so vast and wide,
Lemonade smiles can never hide,
Segmented bliss, our laughter high,
Sweet memories that will never die.

Citrus Dreams in the Making

In the kitchen, chaos breathes,
Fingers sticky, tangy wreaths,
Grandma's recipe written in zest,
But all we want is a juicy quest.

Bobby takes a piece, big and round,
"Look! A treasure I have found!"
But slips and glides, the slickest gem,
Rolls away like a naughty stem.

With every bite, we sing and cheer,
Slurpy giggles, oh so clear,
We crown the fruit a jester now,
With bright orange skin, we'll take a bow.

Citrus dreams dance around our heads,
Utilizing laughter, magic threads,
In the end, it's all a delight,
As we relish in this fruity flight.

The Sweet Tableau

A canvas bright with splashes bold,
Each orb a story waiting to be told,
We gather round for the fruity show,
Laughter spills as we steal the glow.

Little hands reach for the treasure,
Sticky faces, oh what a measure!
Like little artists in a sauce so sweet,
Painting giggles with every neat treat.

The clock ticks, time with zest is grand,
Juice-splattered faces, a merry band,
The tableau shifts with each glee-filled taste,
In this art of joy, there's no time to waste.

As twilight comes, we clean the mess,
The sweet tableau brings happiness,
Memories painted, forever stay,
In this fruity chaos, we will play!

Fragrant Juices of the Day

In the morning light, I found a treat,
A round, bright ball, so juicy and sweet.
I rolled it 'round, it danced with glee,
Its zestful scent was calling me.

With a wink and a twist, I gave it a poke,
The kitchen transformed into a citrus joke.
Sprays flying high, like a lemon surprise,
I laughed as it splashed, right up to my eyes!

A bowl full of laughter, a fruit-filled affair,
Tiny seeds sprouted everywhere!
Each wedge like a grin, each segment a smile,
This goofy task made all the while.

So bring on the sun, let it warm my face,
With orange delights, I found my happy place.
For in every drop, there's a giggle so true,
A morning ritual, fresh and fruity too!

The Color of Citrus Dreams

In the land of dreams where the citrus grow,
There's a rainbow of flavor that steals the show.
With colors so bright, they paint the sky,
Every segment giggles, oh my, oh my!

A tart little fellow meets the sweet, bold king,
They joke and they jive under the sun, they sing.
Juicy jests in each twist; oh what a scene,
A citrus cabaret, like you've never seen!

Dancing on tables, a zesty parade,
Each drop of delight is perfectly made.
So grab a fork, and join in the fun,
Let's make this breakfast a whirl of a run!

With chuckles and chortles, we munch with flair,
Too messy to care, let the juice fly everywhere!
In the color of dreams, where the fun's never done,
You'll always find laughter, when citrus is spun!

Sunlit Wonder in Every Segment

Shining bright under a cheerful sun,
A globe of delight, oh what fun!
With a clever cut, its laughter spills,
In every segment, joy gives thrills.

Tiny droplets dance like stars in the air,
My fingers, a canvas, with zest everywhere.
Each slice a smile, a burst of cheer,
Every bite taken, I giggle in here!

In a sunlit kitchen, the colors unite,
A medley of flavors, a whimsical sight.
I toss it in smoothies, I'll squeeze and I'll squish,
A playful concoction, a citrusy wish!

So here's to the fruit, crowned in delight,
With giggles and grins, we'll feast out of sight.
In every segment, a cautionary tale,
To savor the juice and let laughter prevail!

A Slice of Bliss

In a sunny kitchen, the fun begins,
I take my knife, prepare for whims.
With a slice and a laugh, it's hardly a chore,
As zestful scenes play, I shout, "More! More!"

A fruit of delight, with a cheerful face,
Each cut is precise, yet dances with grace.
Juicy surprises spill out in glee,
Oh the joy of this fruit, as wild as can be!

Let's make a splash, a circus of taste,
With friends and laughter, we won't go to waste.
Each wedge tells a story, oh what a twist,
A slice of pure bliss that you cannot resist!

So grab your forks and let's get to play,
With fruits in our hands, we'll brighten the day.
In this fruity fiesta, we'll dance till we drop,
With smiles so wide, let the laughter not stop!

Pith and Purpose

In the kitchen, chaos reigns,
Citrus warriors on the plains.
Juice flies high, seeds in a dance,
Who knew fruit could take a chance?

With knives held high, we start the show,
Zestful laughter, where did it go?
The pith, a foe, quite bold and brash,
Each cut reveals a juicy splash.

Clumsy hands and cheeky grins,
Orange pulp and playful sins.
Watch out! A slip, a comical fate,
A squirt of juice, oh, isn't it great?

Amid the mess, a treasure found,
Citrus giggles all around.
Our snack, a laugh, with sprays of cheer,
Pith in purpose, fun's volunteer!

Parallels in Flavor

Peeling skin, oh what a sight,
A bright delight, a fruity fight.
Segments shine like little suns,
Battle lines drawn, who has the fun?

With every twist, a giggle bursts,
In this fruity land, we quench our thirsts.
One slice here, a juggling act,
Orange juice, now that's a fact!

Bouncing flavors all around,
In this citrus circus, joy is found.
With zest and laughter, we compare,
How many fruits can we declare?

Tartness meets sweetness in a dance,
We bag the peels with great romance.
Parallels of flavor, all in tune,
Underneath the fun, oranges croon!

Mosaic of Sunshine

Sunshine wrapped in textured skin,
With every slice, the giggles begin.
A mosaic bright, a citrus delight,
    Juicy treasures in the light.

We play the game of fruity darts,
Aiming for smiles, hitting sweet hearts.
Each segment shared, a giddy fling,
A shout for joy, let the laughter ring!

Juicy globes, shining so bold,
In this fruity war, we're never cold.
Seeds take flight like tiny stars,
In our kitchen, we raise the bars!

Orange chuckles fill the air,
A mosaic of joy, without a care.
Sparkling smiles from every bite,
In this sunny feast, all feels right!

The Hidden Sweetness

Beneath the peel, a treasure hides,
A zesty quest, where laughter rides.
With each brave cut, we pull a prank,
Juicy adventures in our tank!

One slice and giggles take to flight,
Juice on our face, what a silly sight!
Orange slices dancing in line,
Sweetness flows, oh how divine!

The pithy tales we weave today,
Each juicy bite leads us astray.
Hidden sweetness on our tongues,
Silly songs of bars and bungs!

With every munch, a laugh erupts,
In this fruity world, joy interrupts.
The hidden sweetness, our shared delight,
In orange dreams, we feel just right!

Morning's Citrus Serenade

In the kitchen, I frolic, with zest in my hand,
The breakfast awaits, plans all unplanned.
Juice spills like giggles, a splash here and there,
Can't find my cup—oh, bother, I swear!

Sunshine's upon us, a bright citrus song,
I dance in the chaos, it won't take long.
With peels like confetti, I leap and I twirl,
Morning's delight makes my head start to whirl.

A Dance of Fragrant Arches

In a whirl of fruit, I prance with delight,
Fragrant arches above, oh, what a sight!
Laughter erupts as I stumble and trip,
Juicy antics abound, not a moment to skip.

The orange rolls away, it's got a mind of its own,
Chasing it down like a dog that has flown.
Round and round we go in a merry chase,
Who knew such fruit could bring smiles to my face!

Threads of Gold and Green

Gold and green threads woven in a grand mess,
Peeling my treasure, oh, what a process!
A sticky tangle, my fingers are trapped,
In citrusy chaos, I find myself wrapped.

A fond memory forms, it gives quite a giggle,
Pulp everywhere, oh, how it does wiggle!
With each cheeky squirt, a burst of pure fun,
A breakfast creation that's second to none!

Tides of Tartness Unfurled

In tidal waves of flavor, I dive with great glee,
Navigating tartness—what a sight to see!
Rolling citrus balls, I juggle with grace,
A fruity circus in this bright, happy space.

I slip and I slide on a juice-covered floor,
That's just what I get for my taste buds to score!
With laughter like ripples, the fun never ends,
In a world made of citrus, we're always the friends.

The Fragmented Sun

The sun is in a twisty peel,
Juices squirt, it's quite surreal.
Bright globes laugh as they roll away,
Chasing shadows, they play all day.

With every twist, a giggle's sound,
The garden's bouncing, round and round.
Little hands dive, a sticky quest,
Finding sunshine in a zestful jest.

Fruits turn tales of summer's cheer,
Each segment holds a tale to hear.
Who knew a fruit could be so spry,
Bouncing laughter as it flies by!

From tree to cheek, in playful glee,
Don't mind the mess, come join with me.
A tangy world where smiles collide,
In fruity fun, let's take a ride!

Where Dreams Burst Open

A peel with flair, it pops and sings,
Inside surprises, joy it brings.
Rubber bands of citrus cheer,
Splashing smiles, oh dear, oh dear!

Laughter echoes, a fruity spree,
Peels like confetti, wild and free.
Dreams don't just rip, they burst with zest,
Refreshing bursts, they are the best!

In a bowl of joy, they dance and play,
With every squeeze, they shout hooray!
Oh fruity friends, so bright and bold,
Your antics are a sight to behold!

We gather round with sticky hands,
Making memories, oh, how it stands!
From kitchen antics to fruity bliss,
In every bite, there's a giggly kiss!

Sweetness Entrapped in Sunshine

In sunny shells, sweet treasures hide,
Joyful bursts with every slide.
Peeling back layers, the giggles grow,
As sweetness drips, and laughter flows.

Fruity faces with laughter bright,
Rolling around in sheer delight.
Hiding in shadows, they plot and scheme,
In a world of citrus, we laugh and dream!

Every bite's a joke, every peel a jest,
Slipping and sliding, oh what a fest!
Under the sun, with friends by the trees,
Life's just sweeter with tangy breeze!

So grab a slice, come join the fun,
Where sweetness glistens, and we all run.
Entrapped in laughter, all ages unite,
With joy as bright as a sunny light!

Daybreak in Fruity Segments

Morning sun on juicy rays,
Peels of gold in cheerful plays.
Segments glisten, all aglow,
Ready to burst in a morning show!

Kickstarting giggles from early dawn,
Fruity slices, come on, come on!
With every twist, a chuckle flies,
Daybreak dances, and laughter rises.

Gather the gang, let's share the fun,
This fruity party has just begun!
Colors collide in a playful view,
As we munch and crunch, it's all brand new!

In fruity segments, the day takes flight,
Every little zest, a pure delight.
So join the feast, let laughter spread,
In this fruity morning, joy is bred!

Vibrance in Each Wedge

In the kitchen, chaos reigns,
Juice splatters like confetti stains.
One for the zesty, one for the sweet,
Each wedge a party, a zany treat.

Peel it back with giggles loud,
The citrus scent draws a merry crowd.
Hands sticky with laughter and zest,
In this fruity fest, we're truly blessed.

We laugh and squirt, it's a shame to waste,
Each drop drips joy like a syrupy haste.
With every wedge, a chuckle we seize,
This orange caper brings us to our knees!

When life gives you rind, take it in stride,
Each juicy slice, a silly ride.
So grab a knife and cut up the fun,
In this vibrant citrus, we're never done!

Peeling Back Layers of Light

Fruits on the counter, they look so bright,
Ripening dreams in the morning light.
With a twist and a turn, we pull back the skin,
Watch out for juice; let the laughter begin!

Like a magician, with a flick of my wrist,
I unveil the segments, oh what a twist!
They giggle and jostle, a zesty surprise,
The scent of sunshine, the taste that defies.

One sip can send you on a tangy spree,
A citrus delight, as wild as can be.
Slips of sweetness dance on the tongue,
In this juicy game, we're forever young!

Layers revealed, and we play the game,
Each slice, a riddle, not quite the same.
So peel back the layers, let's bask in the light,
In this merry mess, everything feels right!

Essence of a Tangy Dawn

Morning surprises in a bowl set low,
Glistening orbs putting on a show.
A squeeze of delight, a splash of cheer,
Brightening spirits as the day draws near.

Wedges awake, with a giggle or two,
Dancing in sunlight, a lively crew.
With every bite, zesty laughter flows,
In this morning ritual, joy simply grows.

Quick wit and juice, what could be more?
The essence of dawn, we simply adore.
Each tangy burst a reason to play,
Lemonade dreams carry us away!

In cheerful abandon, we feast with glee,
Quips and giggles as bright as can be.
So let's raise a toast to the zest we share,
In life's fruity banquet, we're all debonair!

Sun-Kissed Halves

Two halves of laughter, each one a prize,
Beneath the sun, they twinkle and rise.
Bright orange smiles with sparkle and glee,
In the citrus festival, we're wild and free!

Take a big bite, let the fun commence,
A tangy explosion, well, that just makes sense!
With each juicy squirt, we double the cheer,
Sun-kissed delights that we all hold dear.

Rind and fruit dance in merriment bright,
We juggle the pieces, it's pure delight.
In this sunlit kitchen, we're silly sprites,
Creating sweet chaos on lazy good nights.

So here's to our feast, as zesty as gold,
With stories and laughter, a joy to behold.
As we share each half, let's savor and cheer,
In the fruity playground, it's always a year!

The Heart of a Golden Sphere

A golden sphere lay on the floor,
It called to me, 'Come, explore!'
I grabbed a knife, oh what a sight,
This game of food brings pure delight!

With a twist and a turn, I made my plan,
Like a stealthy fruit ninja, I ran!
Bouncing juice flew, a citrus spray,
While giggles erupted in a bright ballet!

A splash here, a splat there, what a mess!
Fruits in combat, I must confess.
With the juice of life, I danced around,
In this zesty circus, laughter abound!

Yet in the end, we shared a toast,
To the heart of a sphere we love the most.
So cheers to the fruit with its sunny glow,
And all the fun that comes, you know!

Juicy Whispers of Nature

In the garden, secrets bloom,
Juicy whispers dispel the gloom.
Nature's giggle, sharp and bright,
Fruits chuckle in the soft sunlight.

I strolled past trees, with a grin so wide,
Hoping for a juicy ride.
The wind teased, 'What will you find?'
With each step, silliness entwined!

I plucked a fruit, oh, what a catch!
It slipped away, like a sneaky match.
Round and round, we played a game,
Nature laughed, and I was to blame!

At last, I caught it, my prize, how sweet!
Juicy whispers turned to a treat.
Together we danced, in a fruity sway,
In a world where laughter always plays!

The Slice of a Summer Day

On a summer day, the sun beamed bright,
I thought of a fruit, a funny sight.
So I grabbed my knife with a trusty cheer,
Determined to conquer, my mission clear!

As I approached, I felt a thrill,
Like a daring knight on a juicy hill.
With a chop and a hop, what a clatter,
The juice erupted, oh, what a scattering!

Friends gathered round, with eyes that gleamed,
Their laughter flowed, as I wildly dreamed.
'Let it rain, let it squirt,' I cried with glee,
A citrus shower, for you and me!

So as the sun set, we'd reminisce,
About juicy antics and happiness.
Each slice was a memory, shared with flair,
A summer day filled with laughter in the air!

Colorful Reflections on a Plate

A plate so bright, a colorful sight,
With fruits arranged, oh what a delight!
Each piece danced in harmony,
A fruity fiesta, just wait and see!

With a wink and a twist, I took a chance,
On this edible art, we began to dance.
The oranges giggled as I took my knife,
Creating a mess, the joy of life!

An explosion of flavors, what a burst!
With laughter and juice, I was well-rehearsed.
Friends gathered 'round, their jaws dropped low,
As I donned an apron, the fruit went to show!

So here's to the colors, the smiles that spread,
On a simple plate, where laughter led.
Each slice a story, a tasty parade,
In this joyful feast, memories are made!

The Simplicity of Citrus Delight

Peeling away that sunny skin,
Juice drips down, let the chaos begin!
Fingers sticky, who needs a napkin?
Citrus smiles, here comes the grin.

Lemon jests with a funky twist,
Lime joins in, you can't resist!
Grapefruit roars with a guffaw loud,
All together, they make a crowd.

A fruit bowl stands in pure dismay,
As I juggle and toss without delay.
A citrus comedy, oh what a play!
Vitamin C has come out to play!

So grab a slice, share the cheer,
Juicy laughter, let's persevere!
In the kitchen, the fun's not done,
With every bite, we're the chosen ones!

Liquid Gold in a Bowl

Liquid sunshine in a bright glass,
Is it a drink or a sweet sassy sass?
Slurping it down, like a kid in class,
In this wild fruit rodeo, I'm the brass!

Fruit salad fun, each color a blast,
Twirling spoons, oh, this day goes fast!
I toss in berries, a colorful cast,
But the zesty citrus steals the vast.

A splash here, a sprinkle there,
Between my giggles, nothing compares.
I sip like a diva, tossing my hair,
While my friends argue about the best pears.

In this juicy world, let's make a bet,
Over who's the juiciest, don't you fret!
With laughter afloat, we'll never forget,
That liquid gold is our goofiest get!

Aroma of Heaven's Orchard

In the kitchen, a citrusy breeze,
Like a jester teasing, with perfect ease.
Tangerines dancing, oh, what a tease!
Scent of the orchard, oh, how it frees.

Zesty giggles waft through the air,
Like pranksters plotting, with flair to spare.
Tart and sweet, a mischievous pair,
An army of fruits, this kitchen's fair!

Lemons chuckle in their sunny attire,
As I prepare this citrus choir.
In every zest, there's laughter to inspire,
With each squeeze, my spirits rise higher!

So come, my friends, let's have a ball,
We'll laugh and play, and never fall.
For every slice is a funny brawl,
In this orchard's magic, we'll stand tall!

Chasing the Morning's Essence

Morning light spills on my breakfast plate,
With vibrant fruits, it's a citrus state.
Juicy laughter as I gleefully sate,
Each bite a burst, oh, what a fate!

Orange cubes, like little suns,
Hiding on toast, playing runs.
I chase them down, the morning fun,
In this fruit race, I'm never outdone.

Pink grapefruit giggles while I slice,
Daring me to make a sugar device.
But each squeeze and squirt rolls like dice,
In this wild breakfast, I'm paying the price!

So join the chase, don't hesitate,
For fruity mornings, we celebrate.
With every tang, we stimulate,
Chasing the essence, no need to wait!

Vivid Segments

Peeling back the sunshine, oh what a sight,
Juicy laughter bursts, a playful bite!
Segments tumble, giggles take flight,
Sticky fingers dance in pure delight.

Each slice a treasure, bright and round,
Citrus jokes about the zesty sound.
With every wedge, a chuckle is found,
Juicy puns my friends have crowned.

Pulp and zest make a merry mix,
Zingy humor, oh what a fix!
A citrus war, with fruity tricks,
Life's a laugh with citrus kicks!

In bowls of laughter, we gather near,
With zesty banter, we toast and cheer!
Orange dreams hang with no fear,
Taste the joy, let's spread some cheer!

Essence of the Grove

In the grove where tangy tales bloom,
Orange giggles shatter the gloom.
Nature's laughter fills every room,
With zest in the air, we make our zoom!

Beneath the leaves, they tumble about,
Citrus secrets are what it's about.
Juicy whispers turn into a shout,
As we roll the fruit, there's no doubt!

Wedges collide, a citrus clatter,
Laughter erupts, oh, how we scatter!
In sweet chaos, our hearts do chatter,
With every slice, more fun does matter!

Sunny rays beam down with glee,
Tickling our souls, so joyfully free.
In a grove of jokes, we climb each tree,
Extracting fun—come join and see!

Sunlit Mandarins

Beneath the sun, they shine so bright,
Mandarins caught in playful light.
With zestful whispers, we take our bite,
Silly smiles spark the sheer delight.

Orange balls bound like kids at play,
Juices flow, and troubles sway.
We toss them 'round in a fruity ballet,
Nature's sugar cure for any malaise.

Fruity feuds in lively rounds,
Peels fly like confetti on the grounds.
Laughter echoed through the sounds,
In this section, cheer abounds!

Squeeze the joy right from the rind,
In every chunk, fun's intertwined.
Together we munch, our spirits aligned,
In this zesty world, happiness we find!

Textures of Tenderness

In the orchard of giggles, we find our place,
Soft skins inviting, with a friendly face.
Tender moments in every space,
Each orange slice, a warm embrace.

Pitting against each other with play,
Juicy laughter brightens the day.
Citrusy puns come out to stay,
In our fruity games, we're light as clay.

Sticky sweetness, oh what a plight,
We juggle the fruit, what a sight!
The joy of these flavors feels so right,
In our citrus world, we take flight!

Chasing the sun, we giggle and roll,
Together we meld, filling the bowl.
In this tender dance, we reach our goal,
With zestful hearts and a playful soul!

Rapture of Rind

In the kitchen, tools align,
With a wink and a grin, I feel fine.
Peeling back layers, oh what a chore,
Juicy bits fly—what a score!

Splashes of zest on my cheek,
Citrus confetti, oh what a freak!
Laughter erupts with each goofy slip,
This fruit fight? A hilarious trip!

Seeds start to dance, oh what a scene,
A juice fountain bursts, it's a citric dream!
Slipping and sliding, fruits in a whirl,
Who knew oranges could make such a swirl?

At last, with a smirk, I take a bite,
Sweet tangy goodness—a pure delight!
With citrus laughter in the air,
I've turned a simple task into a fair!

Burst of Juicy Secrets

In the fridge, a treasure awaits,
A round ball of sunshine that elates.
Peel it slow, oh what a tease,
With every twist, my antics please!

Juice flies high, a citrus burst,
I giggle as it quenches my thirst.
The kitchen's my stage for a fruity dance,
With every slice, I take a chance!

Each segment gleams with secrets untold,
Through slippery hands, my grip grows bold.
I juggle them high with an orange cheer,
Who knew this fruit could bring such jeer?

As I savor the sweetness, laughter rings,
An orange's joy, oh, the fun it brings!
In a zesty mess, I find my glee,
Who knew fruit could be so free?

The Orange's Whisper

In my palm, a vibrant hue,
It whispers tales, both sweet and true.
I talk back, what a silly game,
This fruity banter, my claim to fame!

Peeling layers, oh the thrill!
With every twist, the juices spill.
A citrus giggle that's hard to ignore,
A comedy show from this bright orange core!

I roll it 'round, a joyful dance,
It teases me with every chance.
A slice, a squirt—my face, oh dear!
I'm laughing alone while my friends cheer!

With zest on my shirt, no shame to wear,
It's a laugh-out-loud fruit affair!
Each drop of juice, a funny tale,
In this fruity fun, I shall prevail!

Juicy Reflections

In my kitchen, a vibrant show,
An orb of gold, with a citrus glow.
With a slice and a giggle, I make my mark,
The fruit ballet—it's off the chart!

Juice leaps high, a playful spray,
I look like a mess, come what may.
But laughter echoes in the air,
As I embrace this juicy affair!

The rind's my stage, the knife, my sword,
In this citrus battle, I'm never bored.
With silly faces, we dance about,
Who knew making juice could bring such clout?

Through all the spills, I find delight,
Each slice of laughter, a pure insight.
In juicy reflections, we share the fun,
Who knew this fruit could outshine the sun?

Treasures Concealed in Rind

In a sunny kitchen, bright and loud,
An orange sat, oh so proud.
Peel me, they said, it's not a chore,
But I wrinkled up, like a careful door.

With nimble fingers, they made a twist,
Each slice revealed a citrus mist.
A silly squirt shot across the floor,
And laughter danced as we begged for more.

The juicy gems, all plump and bold,
Were treasures twinkling, pure as gold.
We tasted sunshine in every bite,
And sang silly songs, a goofy delight.

Oh, hidden secrets wrapped in zest,
An orange smiles, it's simply the best!
With seeds like secrets, stories untold,
This fruit's a tale that never gets old.

Symphony of Citrus Notes

In the fruit bowl, an ensemble awaits,
With zestful rhythms and playful traits.
A citrus symphony begins to play,
As peels pirouette in a jazzy display.

Fingers dance like they've lost their mind,
While segments tumble, so unrefined.
The aroma swirls like a sweet ballet,
As giggles erupt, come what may.

We slice through whispers, a citrus tune,
That brightens the mood like a warm afternoon.
Each drop of juice is a note in the air,
A sticky situation, we all share.

With citrus giggles, we cheer and toast,
To juice-filled laughter, we'll never boast.
In this fruity concert, joy takes the lead,
Orange melodies fulfilling our need.

The Golden Embrace at Twilight

In the fading glow of a twinkling hour,
An orange waits, a citrus flower.
It's golden hue, a cheeky surprise,
Hiding sweetness behind its guise.

As twilight beckons, we venture near,
To unveil the joy, shed every fear.
With a twist and a turn, the magic breaks,
And laughter spills, as the juice slakes.

In that golden embrace, flavors collide,
We giggle and munch, let joy be our guide.
Oh, sticky fingers and happy grins,
In this twilight dance, everyone wins.

As shadows lengthen, we feast with glee,
In the sun's last kiss, it's wild and free.
With every segment, the night feels right,
Under a canopy of stars so bright.

Refreshing Revelations Await

In the fridge, a surprise awaits,
An orange, bright, that contemplates.
Will it be juice or a silly game?
With a squeeze of fate, it can't be tame!

The bold zest whispers, "Come take a chance!"
As we chop away, slicing in a dance.
Juicy streams burst, and laughter rings,
Revealing all the joy that it brings.

What fun it is to discover the taste,
With sticky fingers, there's no time to waste.
A fruity puzzle, pieces everywhere,
With zany antics, we simply don't care!

A citrus comedy, sweet and bright,
Refreshingly funny, what a delightful sight.
In every bite, a giggle laced,
In the joy of fruit, our worries erased.

www.ingramcontent.com/pod-product-compliance
Lightning Source LLC
Chambersburg PA
CBHW062112280426
43661CB00086B/564